MARION SANTOS

The Science of Dying Happily

A Simple Guide to a Good Death

First edition

This book was professionally typeset on Reedsy.

Find out more at reedsy.com

Contents

Description

The Science of Dying Happily is about living as well as possible for as long as possible and adapting successfully to change.

Packed with extraordinarily helpful insights and inspiring true stories, award-winning journalist Marion santos shows how to thrive in later life (even when coping with a chronic medical condition), how to get the best from our health system, and how to make your own “good death” more likely. Marion explains how to successfully age in place, how to make your death a sacred rite of passage rather than a medical event. This handbook of preparations—practical, communal, physical, and spiritual—will help you make the most of your remaining time, be it decades, years, or months.

Actively planning for a good death (Caring for the soul)

It’s not necessary to go through a rigorous procedure to get ready to die. It does, however, play a role in each of our lives. By taking the proper precautions, you may ensure that your loved ones will be at ease when you pass away as well as yourself.

It’s never too soon to plan and gather significant life archives.

Such development care arranging tells friends and family and medical care suppliers your desires in regards to clinical consideration if anytime you can’t communicate your needs. Without these orders, groups of friends and family frequently experience a lot of uneasiness and stress in endeavoring to simply decide, making a troublesome time much more troublesome.

Taking care of your issues may not be the most energetic assignment, but rather you’ll feel incredible solace and fulfillment whenever you’ve made it happen. Life is flighty, and beginning planning is rarely too soon.

As we're reaching the finish of life, it's vital to have a period where we say, "OK, I am passing on. It's anything but an issue of if, it's an issue of when. How might I best do that? Would I like 1

to be in the medical clinic? Would I like to be in concentrated care? Do I need them beating on my chest when my heart at last stops? Would I like to simply have solace care or would I like to be home with my family around me?"

In the event that we don't go with the choice to pick the last option, the default of medication will be to simply continue to go, to do another thing. And afterward, we don't get into conversations with our family, we don't have a conclusion, and we pass on as a battle to the completion.

To make this errand as straightforward and simple as could really be expected, we've framed precisely the exact thing that ought to be finished to plan for the finish-of-life process: Decide a Power of Attorney

Legal authority (POA) gives someone else the option to follow up for your sake after you pass — or even before you pass on the off chance that you can't go with choices yourself because of mental or actual inadequacy. Your POA ought to be somebody you trust significantly, as they'll be responsible for all your legitimate and monetary issues after you pass.

Most frequently, the POA is a life partner, relative, or dear companion. It's likewise suggested that you pick a backup POA on the off chance that the first individual doled out as the POA can't satisfy the obligations.

The jobs of the POA contrast in light of the state where you live and the regulations that get there. Ensure you and your POA grasp the subtleties and the public authority necessities of filling in as a medical services specialist.

Set up an Advance Directive - The Living Will A development mandate is a composed assertion itemizing 2

ACTIVELY PLANNING FOR A GOOD DEATH (CARING FOR THE SOUL) your desires in regard to clinical treatment. The most widely recognized advance order is a Living Will, which is a record that guarantees your desires will be followed regardless of whether you can't convey them.

The more prominent the detail in your Living Will, the more probable it is that your desires will be done. A portion of the conceivable consideration choices to address in a Living Will include:

* Revival

* Tube taking care of

* Mechanical ventilation

* Organ gift

* Palliative consideration

Put Away Funding to Pay for Funeral Costs, and Be Specific About the Details

The typical expense of a memorial service these days is generally $6,500. Saving an asset for burial service costs and having an arrangement concerning how these assets ought to be distributed and by whom will limit weight on friends and family.

Be unequivocal about the subtleties: Do you like to be covered or incinerated? In the event that you wish to be covered, has your entombment plot been bought, and where is it found? In the event that you haven't picked an entombment plot, where might you want to be covered? Where will the help be held?

What sort of tombstone or grave marker could you like?

After the subtleties are not set in stone, generally gauge the expenses and put away cash to take care of these expenses when the opportunity arrives. Investigate prepaying for all courses of action, and ensure your friends and family know everything has 3

been paid ahead of time assuming that is the situation.

Make certain to Have a last will A Last Will and Testament determine the destiny of all your genuine property, trusts, and effects. It additionally names the individual (Executor) responsible for completing your desires as depicted in your Will. The more resources and recipients you have, the more crucial it is to have a Will. Having a nitty gritty Will make life a lot simpler for your family and guarantees that no disarray about resources and genuine property distribution emerges after your passing.

There are various sorts of Wills. The absolute most normal are:

Proportional/shared - Reciprocal Wills are in many cases involved by wedded couples or soul mates as a basic method for tying down the exchange of property to the next companion/accomplice upon death. Corresponding Wills between mates is essentially perfect representations of each other. In a corresponding Will, every mate/accomplice passes on all or most of their home to the next.

• Spiritualist - A Will that stays fixed until the individual's passing.

• Unsolemn - A Will where the agent stays obscure or anonymous.

• Holographic - A transcribed Will that should be endorsed the hard way and have all material terms composed by the deceased benefactor.

• Serviceman - The desire of an individual to take part in well-trained military help.

A Will can be set up by a legal counselor, by utilizing an internet-based structure, or essentially by the individual one-4

ACTIVELY PLANNING FOR A GOOD DEATH (CARING FOR THE SOUL) self. The main perspectives to cover incorporate choosing the recipients (who gets what), picking the Executor (counting whether that individual will get remuneration for their work), and picking a watchman assuming wards are an element.

Coordinate Finances, Life Insurance, Bills, and Debts Reports that are fundamental for spreading the word to relatives before you pass are any extra security arrangements and retirement plans. These resources are frequently neglected on the grounds that Executors and relatives don't understand they exist. Assuming the assets go unclaimed, the State will be the recipient.

Make a rundown of pay sources and resources (benefits, IRA, CDs, 401(k)s, and so forth.). Frame any ongoing speculations (counting properties) and detail any current advances. In the event that you have a well-being store box, incorporate the areas of the crate and the key.

On the off chance that you're uncertain whether all parts of your funds are all together, counsel a legal counselor.

Plunk Down with the Power of Attorney and Executor to Discuss Your Will

These two individuals play basic parts to play in your life and your bequest, so it's fundamental to meet with everyone and go over the subtleties of your development orders and Will.

Ensure everyone knows their job and that they comprehend the substance of reports connecting with funds, resources, and end-of-life orders.

Each time a change to your Will is made, contact the POA and Executor to refresh them on the changes.

The POA is limited by the archive the individual endorsed to act as POA and make liability regarding specific moves and choices.

5

THE SCIENCE OF DYING HAPPILY

On the off chance that there's a misconception or the POA isn't sure about what you need, a court might need to choose.

Keep All Relevant Records and Documents in a Master File When every one of the above advances is finished, put the significant reports into an expert document and offer the area with the doled out Executor and Power of Attorney. Significant archives that ought to be kept in this record include:

* Last Will and Testament

* Rundown of resources

* Birth declaration

* Marriage declaration

* Identification

* Driver's permit

* Letter of Instruction with respect to insights concerning your burial service, elaboration on parts of your Living Will, and so forth.

* Separate/partition papers

* Government-backed retirement number

* Rundown of pay sources

* Composed trust

* Vehicle title

* Mortgage holder deeds

2

Making Aging Simpler (making peace with loss)

Every person has an own interpretation of what a simple life is and what it is worth. For me, it entails reducing your life to the bare minimum, choosing calm over chaos, and devoting the majority of your time to the things that matter to you. Knowing your priorities is the first step to simplifying your life.

Simplifying your life allows you to spend more time with the people you cherish and doing the things you like. Getting rid of the excess stuff will leave you with only the things that are truly valuable.

It’s not always easy to arrive at simplicity, though. There is no destination; it is a journey. objective, and it can frequently be an excursion of two steps in the right direction, and one in reverse.

Instructions to Simplify Your Life In the event that you’re keen on improving your life, this is an extraordinary starter’s aide.

For the critics who say that the rundown underneath is 7

excessively lengthy, there are truly just two moves toward improving:

1. Identify what means quite a bit to you.

2. Eliminate all the other things.

Obviously, that is not horribly valuable except if you can perceive how to apply that to various aspects of your life, so I present to you the Long List.

There can be no comprehensive bit-by-bit manual for work on your life, however, I've arranged a deficient rundown of thoughts that ought to help anybody attempting to track down the basic life. Few out of every odd tip will work for you — pick the ones that allure and apply to your life.

One significant note: this rundown will be reprimanded for being excessively muddled, particularly as it gives a lot of connections. Try not to worry about pretty much all of that.

Simply pick each in turn, and spotlight on that. At the point when you're finished with that, emphasize the following thing.

1. Make a List of Your Top 4-5 Most Important Things Does that mean quite a bit to you? What do you esteem most?

What 4-5 things do you most maintain that should do in your life? Improving begins with these needs, as you are attempting to make room in your life so you possess more energy for these things.

2. Assess Your Commitments

See all that you have happening in your life: work, home, children's exercises, leisure activities, side organizations, individual tasks, and so forth. Contemplate which of these truly gives you esteem, and which ones you love doing.

Which of these are in accordance with the 4-5 most significant things you recorded previously? Drop those that aren't in accordance with those things.

3. Assess Your Time

How would you go through your day? What things do you do, from the time you awaken to the time you nod off?

Make a rundown, and assess whether they're in accordance with your needs. In the event that not, dispose of the things that aren't, and center around what's significant. Overhaul your day.

4. Improve on Work Tasks

Our work day is comprised of a perpetual rundown of work assignments. On the off chance that you essentially attempt to knock off every one of the assignments on your plan for the day, you won't ever finish everything, and more terrible yet, you won't ever finish the significant stuff. Center around the fundamental assignments and kill the rest.

5. Work on Home Tasks

Along those lines, contemplate all the stuff you do at home.

Some of the time our home errand list is similarly the same length as our work rundown, and we won't ever finish that all things considered. Zero in on the most significant, and attempt to track down ways of dispensing with different errands (robotize, kill, representative, or recruit help).

6. Limit Your Options

Some portion of living just is to limit your need to immense decisions on the day-to-day. A few things may honestly be superfluous.

Take a gander at your plan for the day and wipe out errands that are not significant, and check whether you can mass a few things together. Having a long plan for the day can be overpowering, and be careful that our energy is limited.

7. Time Blocks

As a business person, time extravagance can some of the time feel more like a revile than a gift. Set working hours for yourself, 9

particularly with regards to finishing individual tasks.

Obstructing your timetable or setting time periods to finish explicit jobs can assist with keeping you on target without being enticed by outside interruptions. This is a method for telling your cerebrum when now is the right time to work and when now is the ideal time to loosen up, and it's exceptionally useful in improving your everyday existence.

8. Set up the Night Before

Dispose of superfluous errands by setting up your things the prior night. Despite the fact that it could take you ten minutes to accumulate your work things in the first part of the day, why not make it happen the prior night and utilize that additional chance to ponder or peruse the paper? Working on your life additionally requires using your time better.

9. Set Your Rhythm

Each day, we pursue the cognizant choice of establishing our rhythm for the afternoon. Recall a second when you had gotten up behind schedule for work and felt bothered and overpowered.

Your activities and responses play like domino pieces, which either raise or bring down your vibrations. While you're having a terrible day, ordinarily brought about by one thing influences another, etc.

By being deliberate about your speed, you have the control to stop at any second to step back and reset. Get your early daytime going right by deliberately concluding how your day will unfurl.

10. Find What Works for You

There are numerous ways of adjusting your financial balances.

What works for you may not work for someone else, and the extraordinary thing about present-day innovation is the wealth of uses that are promptly accessible on your PC or telephone.

11. Stress Only When Needed

10

MAKING AGING SIMPLER (MAKING PEACE WITH LOSS)
This one will take some training. In the event that we're not aware of our viewpoints, our concerns can go with us over the course of the day.

There are ways of being proactive when the considerations begin collapsing, for example, making the opportunity to stress and just concerned. While doing this training, you'll start to acknowledge how long and energy is spent agonizing over specific things and how dreary a portion of these concerns might be.

Whether it be 5 minutes or 15 minutes, invest that energy tending to those concerns and leave those concerns there when that time is up.

15. Limit Your Communications Our lives these days are loaded up with a huge progression of correspondences: email, IM, cells, paper mail, Skype, Twitter, and discussions, and that's only the tip of the iceberg. It can require up your entire day assuming that you let it.

All things being equal, set a boundary for your correspondences: just email at specific times, for a specific number of minutes. Limit calls to specific times, as well. Set a timetable and stick to it.

Improving your life is tied in with zeroing in on what means a lot to you. It's tied in with finding simpler ways of doing the things that you need to do and giving yourself more wriggle space for the things you need to do.

Effortlessness is certainly not an enchanted wand for a simple life, yet as far as I can tell, it most certainly makes things more straightforward.

11

3

CHANGE ADAPTATION (practicing interdependence)

We change from the moment we are born onward. Our bodies and minds never stop changing to fit the environment we live in. Although there may be restrictions and losses as we age, the aging process is progressive. When you acknowledge how much time has passed, you could be shocked.

You also have company because everyone is aging at the same time. Relationships with people who have gone through similar things in life can be comforting and uplifting.

Many retirees have eagerly anticipated this time in their lives when they are free from the obligations of a career and having children.

We are better able to adjust to the problems that may come our way as we get older, which is one of the benefits of aging.

Additionally, we learn that now is not the moment.

Adjusting to changes that age can bring 1. Your cardiovascular framework 12

CHANGE ADAPTATION (PRACTICING INTERDEPENDENCE) Your veins and conduits can start to solidify, making your heart work harder.

What you can do:

·Make actual work a piece of your day-to-day everyday practice

·Eat a solid eating regimen

·Try not to smoke

·Oversee pressure

·Get sufficient rest

2. Bones, joints, and muscles Bones can become more fragile and more vulnerable to crack.

Loss of muscle strength, perseverance, and adaptability can likewise happen, influencing your equilibrium and dependability.

What you can do:

·Get sufficient measures of calcium and vitamin D

·Add actual work to your everyday daily schedule to construct, serious areas of strength for muscle and further develop balance 3. Your memory and thinking abilities You might see minor impacts on your memory or thinking abilities, for example, failing to remember a name or word or you might battle with performing multiple tasks.

What you can do:

·Remember actual work for your day-to-day everyday practice

·Eat a solid eating regimen

·Keep your psyche dynamic

·Be Social

·Oversee cardiovascular gamble factors as they can expand the gamble of mental deterioration 4. Your eyes and ears

You might battle to zero in on objects that are close and become more delicate to glare.

Your hearing could reduce and you might see trouble in hearing high frequencies or following a discussion in a jam-packed room.

What you can do:

·Plan standard tests and heed guidance with respect to whether you want glasses, amplifiers, or other restorative gadgets

·Wear shades or a wide overflowed cap outside and earplugs on the off chance that you're around clearly commotions 5. Your weight

Your digestion dials back and assuming you decline exercises yet keep eating similar measure of calories, you'll put on weight.

What you can do:

·Remember active work for your everyday daily practice

·Eat a solid eating regimen

·Watch your piece sizes

6. Your teeth

Gums could start to pull back and certain drugs can cause a dry mouth, making your gums and teeth somewhat more powerless against rot.

What you can do:

·Clean your teeth two times every day and floss something like one time per day

·Plan normal exams with your dental specialist and hygienist 7. Your skin

As your skin diminishes it turns out to be less versatile and you might wound all the more without any problem. Less normal oils are created so your skin becomes drier.

What you can do:

·Wash or shower in warm water, not hot, with a gentle cleanser and utilize a lotion

·At the point when you're outside, use sunscreen and wear a 14

CHANGE ADAPTATION (PRACTICING INTERDEPENDENCE) defensive dress

A great many people partner advanced age with so many credits as "careless," "ugly," "sick," or "desolate"

these discoveries show the way that more established individuals can apply control and accomplish positive results in any event, when they experience expanding misfortunes related to maturity.

Improvement at whatever stage in life isn't simply a latent course of development and unfurling of capacities and abilities, but a continuous and dynamic connection of an individual with their climate. In this section, we

center around inspirational changes as a critical variable for grasping the variation

process in more seasoned adulthood.

The inspirational

methodology centers around the job of objectives for effective maturing. According to this viewpoint, variation doesn't just include the

change of an individual to changes in the accessibility of inside and outside assets, what's more, requests of the climate, yet in addition, involves that people proactively place themselves and shape their current circumstance as per their objectives. In that capacity, like the use of the term in science, adaption alludes to a course of upgrading the fit

between an individual and the climate when confronted with inner or outside changes.

4

Dealing With Mortality (The final hours) We all struggle with the problem of accepting our mortality.

Accepting death, though, can be quite difficult. Each of us must come to terms with the fact of death in our own manner. But having faith and using common sense can both be helpful.

For instance, acknowledging that life is limited concentrates our attention, allowing us to reflect on our lives and consider the opportunities that lie ahead. We could ponder difficult issues like what kind of impact we want to have on the world. And what do we hope to leave behind?

Passing can't be really perceived. Demise is better perceived inside the spirit, our fundamental being, and our heart. In a culture where kicking the bucket and passing is dreaded, we have no verbal language to communicate the enormity of biting the dust, demise, or pain; no fitness to be an unwavering observer or to grasp how it feels to color. What we most significantly think and trust, what we enthusiastically love, dread, or want, unquestionably gets away from adequate verbalization — likewise with death.

 In this manner, few contemplate how one methodology passing, or lives in dread, having the specific information that demise is standing by. We experience the ill effects of what I call a passing lack of education. We live realizing that everything bites the dust. Like the sun, it's an unavoidable truth. Also, similar to the sun, we tend not to check it out. Except if you've encountered a new passing, it's most likely not something you examine. The feeling of dread toward death torments us like nothing else. Any remaining feelings of trepidation — like public talking, centipedes, and levels — fail to measure up. Thus, we don't actually discuss it. We are in good company; passing has tormented most living spirits over the course of time. For millennia, most old and winning social legends, world religions, and beliefs have helped mankind in seeing such superb secrets of life as the compromise of awareness with death. For over thirty years, I have gone with the perishing to the edge past which they should cross alone. Having had the honor of working with many spirits as a Hospice social laborer, teacher, End of Life Counselor, Death Doula, Ordained Minister, and Founder of The HeartWay, an association committed to Embracing Life through Honoring Death, I have seen the perishing, their families, and their parental figures battle to grasp the great secrets of life through the undeniable methodology of death. For certain, when clients ponder their mortality; partake in discussions with their friends and family, specialists, and confided in companions about their feelings of dread, wishes, and wants about death; and foster a close connection with death — life is changed. Each hallowed brush with death endorses a brief look into the extraordinary secret of this life. I have not found a manual, in spite of the fact that there are many composed, that gives every one of the responses to figuring out the superb secrets throughout

everyday life and demise. Passing on is a domain without any specialists, yet my experience uncovers that you can lessen the enduring by being pretty much as present as conceivable to death and kicking the bucket. Much to be acquired from is being available all through the entirety of our life. I really do realize that individuals experience more mind-boggling pain whenever they have not had the chance to bid farewell, share their adoration, and defy their feelings of dread. The discussion inside the limits of death is a long-lasting relationship and more than can be summarized with words alone.

May we always remember that Death coaxes us to bid farewell, accommodate our connections, see as significance, lament our misfortunes and love one another.

From the journals of my work, I offer you a couple of devices that I keep on using in assisting my clients with getting ready for the difficulties that emerge inside passing on, death, and the sadness that follows:

5

Getting help while actively dying (Saying goodbye)

The dying process culminates in active dying.

The active

stage of dying lasts around three days as opposed to the pre-active stage's approximate three-week duration. Actively dying individuals are, by definition, very close to passing away and display several indications of near-death. For instance, people who are actively dying frequently become unresponsive, and their blood pressure frequently decreases dramatically.

From this educational experience, I modestly offer these 3

Things to recollect at the bedside of a Dying Person for a more hallowed cognizant and thoughtful splitting as the time moves close.

First

Address their Spirit and see their Spirit.

Large numbers of us get overpowered when we see a withering individual. The last time we saw them most likely was at a bubbly occasion. Christmas, Thanksgiving, a wedding, or something more friendly and presently you see them as an actual shell of the

individual they were previously. We can get effortlessly wrecked by this and the differentiation is an excessive amount to take.

Investigate their eyes and utilize your eyes to grin at them.

Send your adoration in your eyes to their eyes. Fill their inward being with the empathy of your heart.

No requirement for words. Large numbers of us will meander aimlessly something to facilitate our own distress in the circumstance. In any case, consider the number of individuals that came in and did likewise to them. That is the reason my mom in her more terrible states would not see any longer. She was unable to talk however motioned for a piece of paper and wrote in a scribbling, “I would rather not see anybody.”

See their soul. Train yourself to recollect them at their best.

Their chuckling, their number one statement, their best dish.

Search for and check their soul out.

Second

Know that what you in all actuality do say might be the last point you make to this individual. You should not have to say the savvies of things. Nobody can be savvier than somebody on the move. They have seen a ton and endured a great deal and found out such a great amount about themselves before they leave. Your errand is to work with smooth and serene progress.

So in your insight and sympathy, be caring with your words.

This isn't an ideal opportunity to go through complaints or to anticipate that significant choices should be made. Similarly, the primary point was to see their soul and address it. I welcome you to carry your own soul to the bedside. Not your insight or your profound hang-ups and stories.

Right now, the majority of life and the set of experiences truly don't make any difference. The most valuable second is to be there and present to one another. Recognizing the amount you 20

GETTING HELP WHILE ACTIVELY DYING (SAYING GOODBYE) both mean to one another. Indeed, there will be tears. These are tears of delights enveloped with distress. It is simply because you mean such a great amount to one another that the splitting could hurt this much.

Third

In any event, when the individual is by all accounts resting or is semi-cognizant and can't answer or appear at an actual level, not to be alert or mindful; their soul and awareness are still there in the room.

A number of us say romantic things to our kids and accomplices as they rest. We lay our eyes with affection on the supernatural occurrence of this individual as he/she dozes.

6

Final summary

Unfortunately, there is a wide range in what many people who are dying experience. Only a third of Medicare patients who request at-home hospice care actually receive it. The number of people who pass away in hospitals, in pain, alone and after a protracted medical battle with an incurable illness is far too high.

Too often, doctors with the best of intentions try ineffectively to extend the lives of terminally ill patients at exorbitant financial and emotional expenses. As bereaved spouses shared tragic experiences replete with tears, fury, remorse, and loneliness in our grief support group, it became clear to me the disastrous effect that kind of death can have on survivors.

22

Document Outline

-
-
-
-
-
-
-

www.ingramcontent.com/pod-product-compliance
Lightning Source LLC
LaVergne TN
LVHW020547160826
845677LV00015B/4251